To my parents, Nicholas and Bettye Karris,
and to my yiayia, Elizabeth Loris Argol,
from whose lips I first heard
"The Lord's Prayer"

Sincerest thanks to His Eminence Archbishop Spyridon,
the Very Reverend Father George Passias, Reverend Father Philemon Sevastiades,
Ann R. Griffin, Patti Paxson, Presvytera Patra McSharry Sevastiades,
Theo Nicolakis, Demetri and Angela Konstantopoulos, and especially to
Reverend Father George Konstantopoulos, my husband, for his loving support
and encouragement throughout these many years.

Published in 1999 by Cappadocia Press, New York.
Copyright © 1999 by Elaine Konstantopoulos.

First Edition

Book and cover design: Ann R. Griffin

Cover photo: © Peter Drakoulias,
courtesy of St. Nicholas Shrine Church, Flushing, NY.

Illustrations:
p. 5 courtesy of Holy Transfiguration Monastery, Brookline, MA;
pp. 15 and 17 painted by monk Michael of the Kellion of the Holy Angels,
Mount Athos, used by permission;
pp. 19 and 27 courtesy of Penelope Byham;
p. 25 courtesy of the Greek Orthodox Archdiocese of America;
all other illustrations from private collections.

ISBN 1-58438-000-4

Manufactured in the United States of America

Cappadocia Press
Imprint of the Greek Orthodox Archdiocese of America
8 East 79th Street, New York, NY 10021
Web site: www.goarch.org

MEDITATIONS ON

The Lord's Prayer

ELAINE KONSTANTOPOULOS

CAPPA
DOCIA
PRESS

NEW YORK

The relationship between God and human being is a mystery. As Orthodox Christians, we believe that Jesus Christ is at the center of Creation. The majesty of Creation resonates to that spiritual center within each of us that seeks to communicate with the Creator. When Jesus Christ was asked how we should pray, He gave us this one and only prayer as the perfect model of communication between us and the Almighty. The Lord's Prayer remains at the center of the Christian prayer experience. I am pleased that this meditation explores some of the deep questions that the Lord's Prayer raises to those who experience its power to transform. For those who contemplate its profound meaning, the Lord's Prayer will connect their innermost soul to the Creator. May all who enter into this mystery feel the love, joy, and peace of the Most High God through the power of the Holy Spirit.

+ Archbishop Spyridon
Primate of the Greek Orthodox Church of America

Christ the Good Shepherd

Our Father,

O Lord, You are our Father. You belong to all, even though there are times when I feel you are mine alone. We all feel that way, I suppose; it is the way a child feels toward his earthly father.

You have made us, and we belong to You — the Father, the Creator, the awesome Power of the universe. When we suffer, we cry to You to soothe our pain. When we know great joy, we turn to You in praise. When we seek advice, we share with You our secrets. And so, You are always the beginning of our prayer.

Who art
in heaven,

Where is heaven, Lord? Is it above? When we were young, we were taught to look up when praying to You. Should we look elsewhere, Lord? Should we look around us to find heaven? Should we look within?

Heaven is where the saints and angels are, O Lord, ready for You to send them to help us. We see the things You have made and therefore know where You have been and what You have touched. Heaven is with You, O Lord. I pray that I will always be close to You, until one day, by Your mercy, I join You — because I cannot imagine life without You.

 Hallowed be
Thy Name.

"Praise the Name of the Lord, for it is good." The psalmist has said it best. Your name is sacred, Lord, and should be uttered only with awe and reverence. When we consider

something sacred, we hold it tenderly and dearly, close to our hearts. It becomes for us the most precious thing in the world ... So is Your Name, Lord — most beautiful, most sacred, most sublime.

 Thy
kingdom
come.

Lord, one day this world with all its problems and difficulties will pass, and all those who have lived will live again forever. A never-ending day will dawn when there will be no sickness — or death — when evil will end forever.

On that day we will see things plainly and be in Your presence eternally. We cannot know when that day may be, Lord. Give us the grace to be ready when it comes.

Thy will be done,
on earth as it is
in heaven.

Why is it so difficult to remember that You are in charge, Lord? You always have been and always will be. Why do we act as if we are in charge? What do we control that is of real significance? Do we control the elements? Can we make a blade of grass grow? Can we  make a bird sing? Can we give life to an embryo, or take the soul into our hands when death beckons? God, help me to put my life back into Your most capable hands. And when I pray, help me not to tell You what to do. Can I tell You how to run the universe? You know what is best. You know our needs even before we ask. Please forgive us when we forget this, O Lord.

 Give us this
day our daily
bread.

Give us only what we need today, Lord. You, better than anyone else, know what we need at any given time. One day it may be bread itself; another day it might be the bread of spiritual nour-ishment satisfying our hungry souls like manna in the desert. One day we may need guidance; one day, compassion; but always we need Your love.

My daily bread is nothing without Your love, O Lord; for it is Your love that truly gives me life.

And forgive us
our trespasses as
we forgive those who
trespass against us.

How can we ask for Your forgiveness, Lord, if we cannot forgive others? Yet we do it all the time! We say, "Lord, please forgive the wrong I have done. I didn't mean it; I will never do it again." At the same time, however, we carry a grudge against someone who has caused us pain.  If You can forgive us, Lord, when we have caused You pain, why can we not forgive another?

You have told us that we must become like You — in every respect. There can be no room in heaven for those who cannot forgive. If we do not love, we are not Your disciples. Help us to learn, Lord, that forgiving is easier than hating and not forgiving. And Lord, as we forgive others, help us to forgive ourselves as well.

And lead
us not into
temptation,

It's all around us, Lord — so much to turn us astray, so much to distract us, so much to lead us away from  You. We know better than to follow these temptations; but sometimes we find it difficult to obey You. When temptations present themselves, we often wander off Your path. We are great justifiers, finding excuses for our sins. We need strength, Lord, to keep to Your path. Shield me, I pray, from every temptation, that I may walk according to Your will and not my own.

But deliver us from the evil one.

Evil does exist, Lord. I know, for I have seen its ugliness. I have seen how it can twist truth and deceive. I have witnessed how it destroys. Deliver me, O Lord, from the snares of such a horrific spirit. Enter my soul, Lord, for You alone are invited to dwell within me. I am Yours, Lord, and on  bended knee I ask You to remain with me. Guard my soul as Your Angel guarded the entrance to the Garden of Eden. Stand at the end of the road so that I may see Your Light and not fear the darkness that surrounds me. Evil can flourish only when we fail to listen to you, when we hear the evil one instead. But deliver me from him, O Lord, now and always — and especially when I leave this world, that I may be delivered straight to You, O loving and holy and all-forgiving Father.

For Thine is the
kingdom, and
the power, and
the glory,

The only true kingdom is Your kingdom. You are the Power, the Energy, the Life Force. It is because of You that all Creation lives and breathes. We humbly kneel before You, our God, for all  the glory we could possibly ever offer is Yours. "The heavens declare Thy glory," and so do we, dear God.

Of the Father, Son,
and Holy Spirit,
now and forever.

"Forever" is a concept impos—
sible for us to comprehend,
Lord. We can grasp only the
finite. For us, all things must
end, but not for You. You
were, are, and always will be.
How awesome a thought!
You are eternal and give each

of us the opportunity to spend eternity with You. Help
me to remember that the steps to eternity begin now.
And guide my footsteps, O Lord, that day by day I
may follow the path that leads to You.

Amen